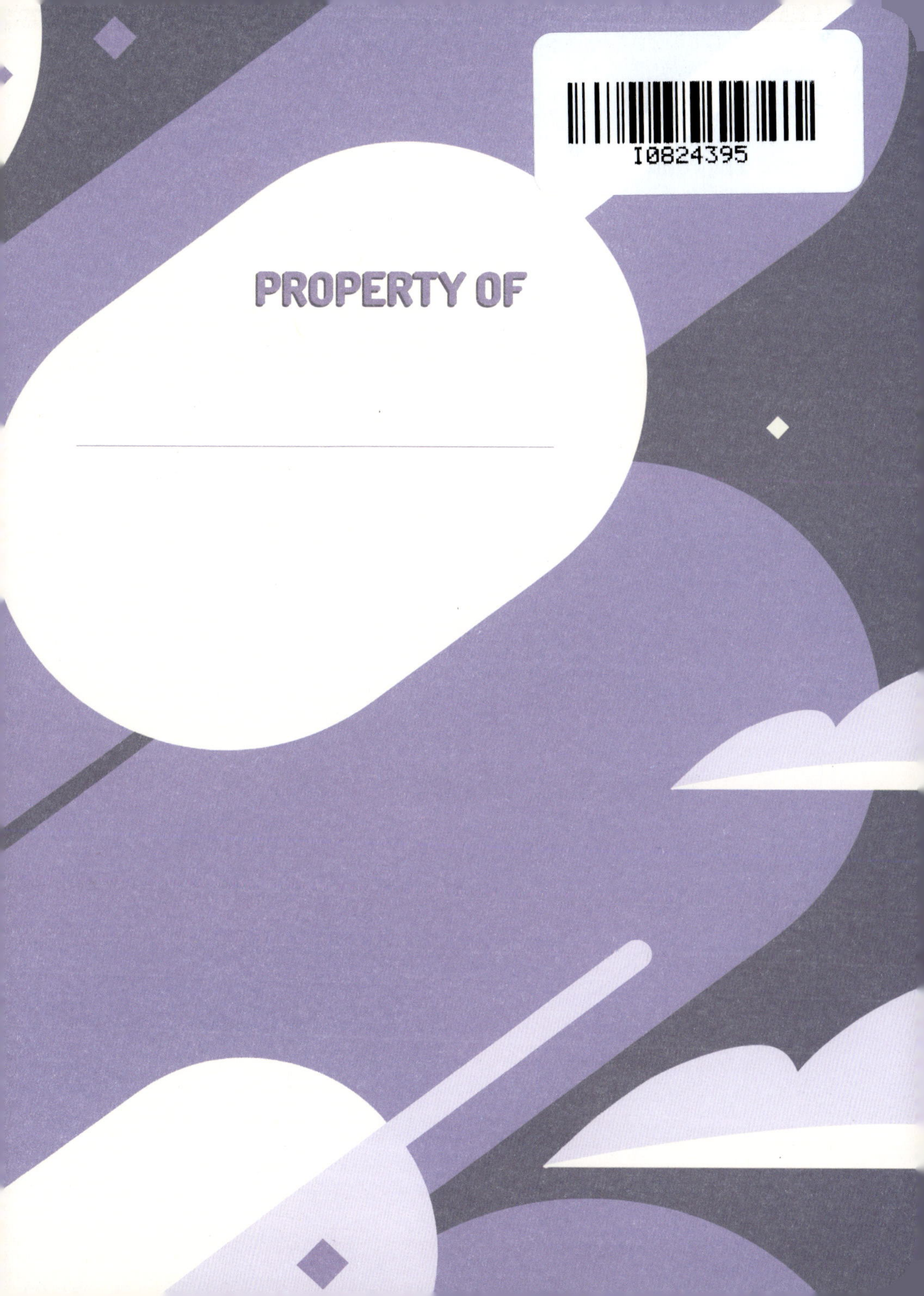
PROPERTY OF

Foreword

My brother Steven and I have been drawing together since we were kids. I'm the older one, so I used to always give him drawing advice, but he ended up giving me the best piece of advice I've ever received. One weekend, when he was in high school, Steven drew a comic all about birds. I was surprised because I'd never seen him draw a bird before. "Why birds?" I asked, and he said, "I didn't know how to draw birds, and now I do."

My mind was blown. I never stopped thinking about this. I started building projects around whatever I wanted to learn how to draw. And I would draw obsessively, redoing drawings over and over until I felt I had perfected whatever I was studying.

Back then I couldn't stand sketchbooks, because every time I made a mistake I would tear it out or abandon the sketchbook for a new one. Eventually I started keeping binders, so I could throw out the majority of my drawings and save only the good ones in sheet protectors. Doing a great drawing, whenever that lightning would strike, made me happier than anything in the world. But doing bad drawings made me miserable . . . so I was miserable most of the time.

Years later, when I started working on *Steven Universe*, I knew it would be the hardest project of my life, and so I chose the lesson I knew would be the hardest to learn. I would need to give up on impossible perfection and let myself make mistakes. I would need to face and accept and share my process drawings with my team. I would need to learn how to keep a sketchbook . . .

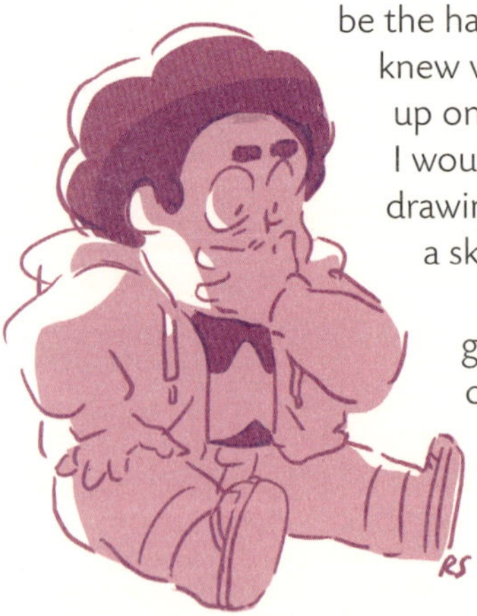

So I stapled a sketchbook together out of literal garbage: scrap paper and pages of magazines and cut-up paper bags. I would draw on receipts, paper tablecloths, and Post-its and tear them up and tape them in. There are so many terrible drawings that are still in there, but in the time I would have

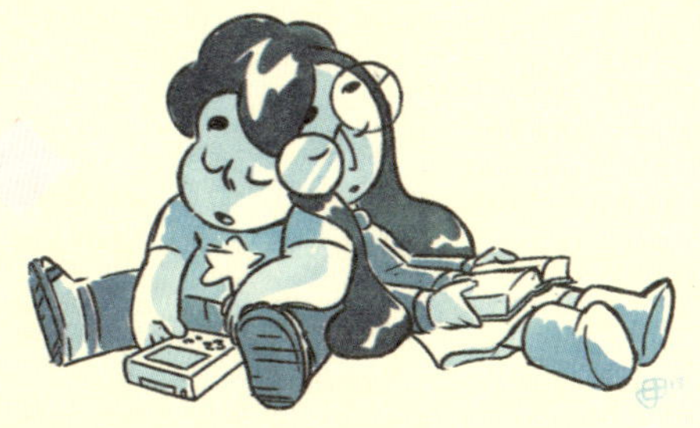

spent agonizing over them, I made more drawings instead. Finally, when that was full, I graduated to an actual sketchbook that I didn't tear apart or throw away. Now there are tons of sketchbooks and drawings floating around our conference room at work, intermingling with other brilliant Crewniverse members' process drawings and doodles, some of which have found their way into this book.

So please, if you share this struggle with me, share this sketchbook with me. Let everything flow out of you, and enjoy the way your mind is discerning "good" and "bad." That ache is the part of you dying to learn something, solidifying priorities, and dreaming of better drawing and a better you. But really, with the power to decide what "better" means and the motivation to get there, you already are that better you. That's what I learned from my wonderful brother.

Yours,
Rebecca Sugar

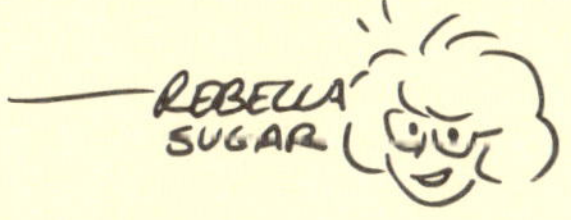

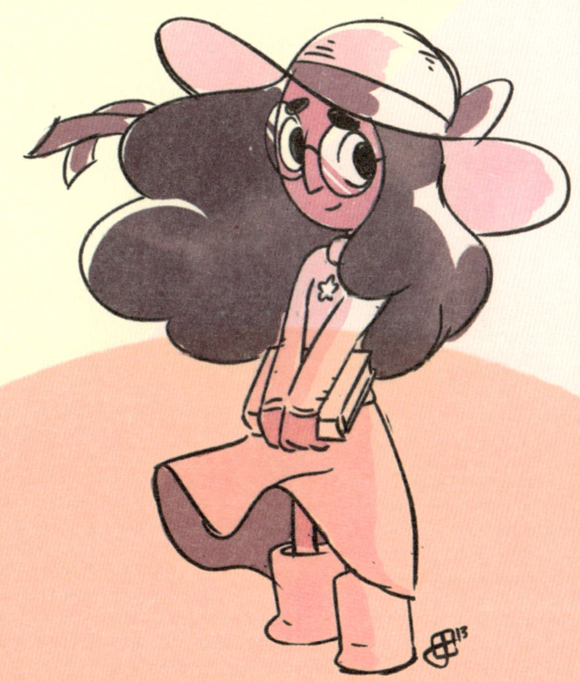

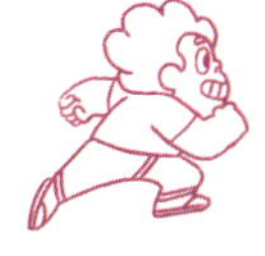

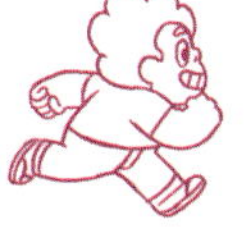

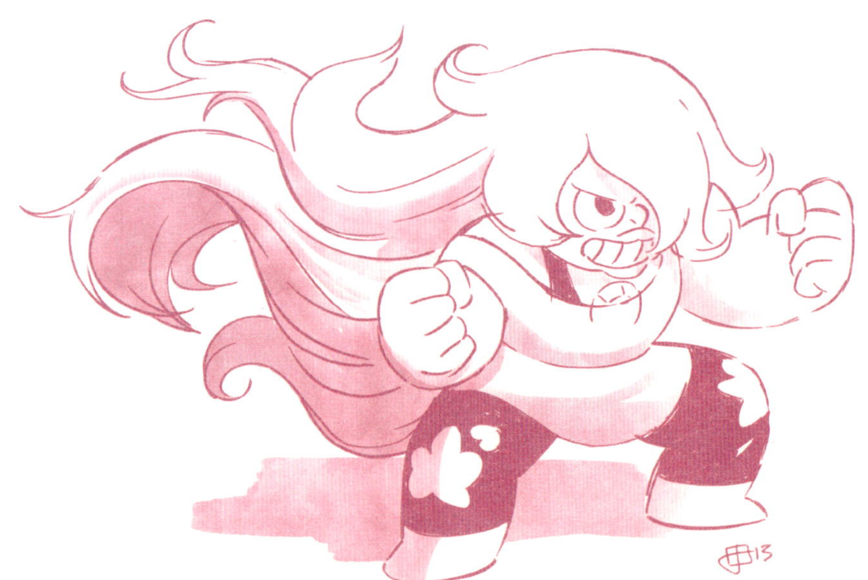

Joe Johnston

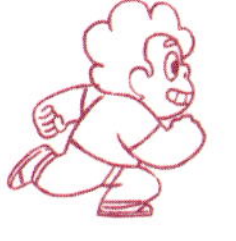

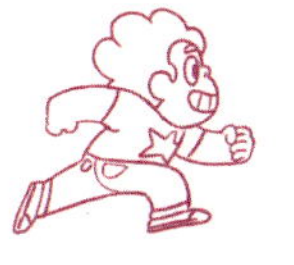

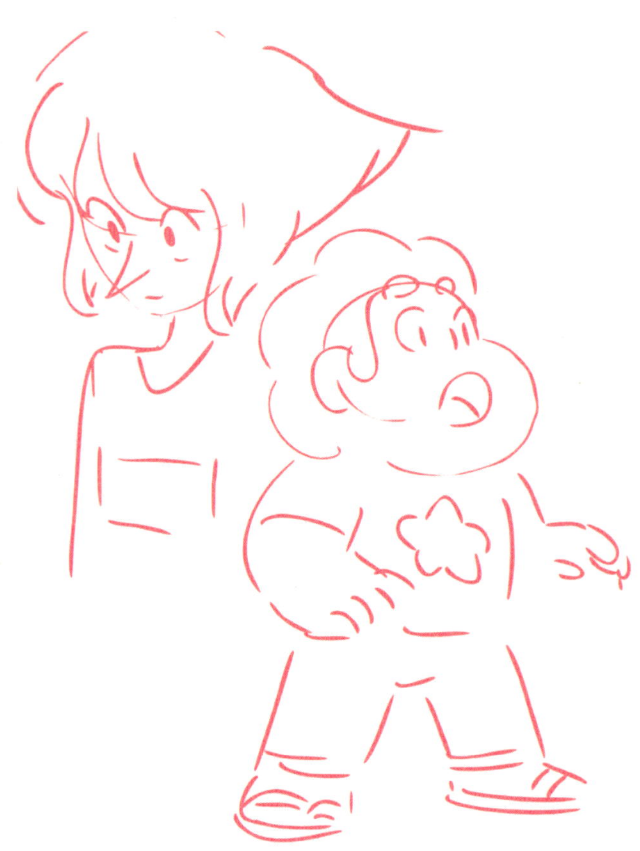

Joe Johnston

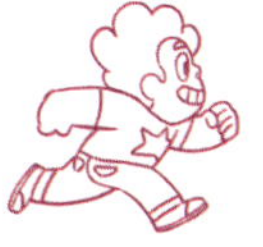

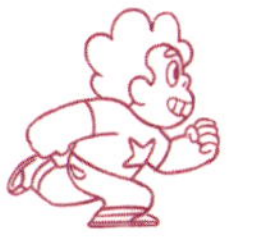

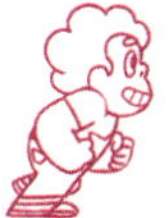

Lamar Abrams

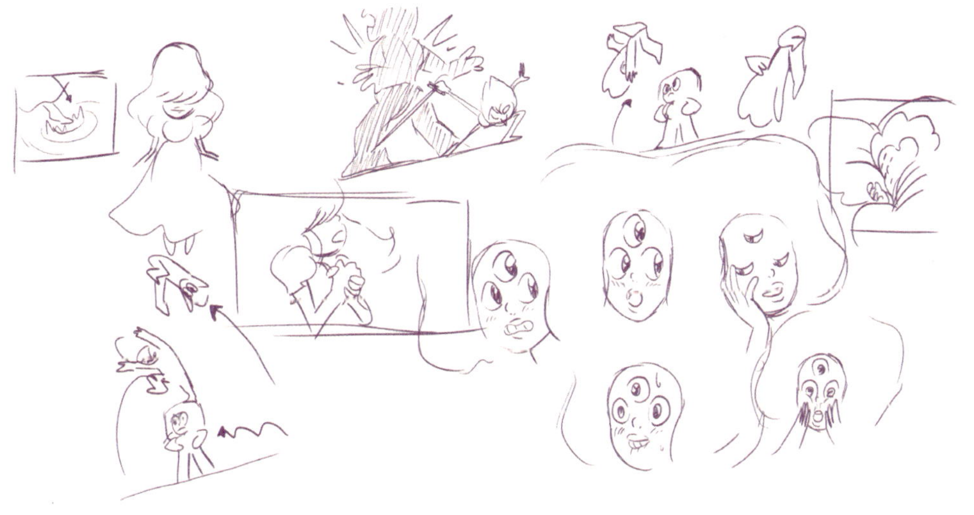

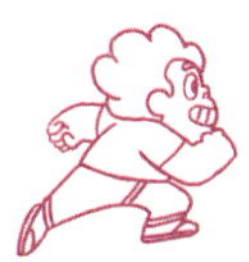

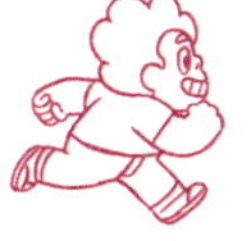

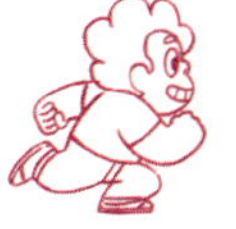

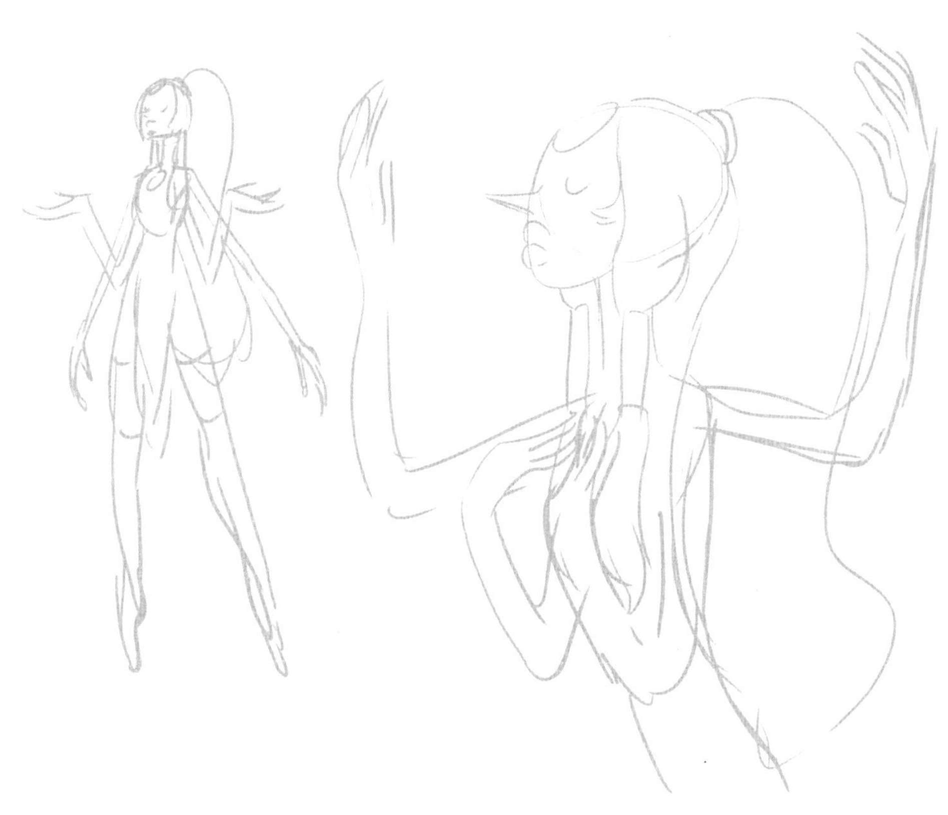

Joe Johnston

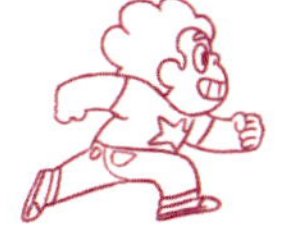

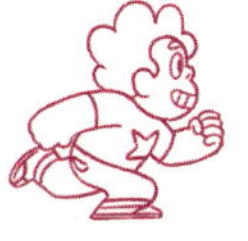

Joe Johnston

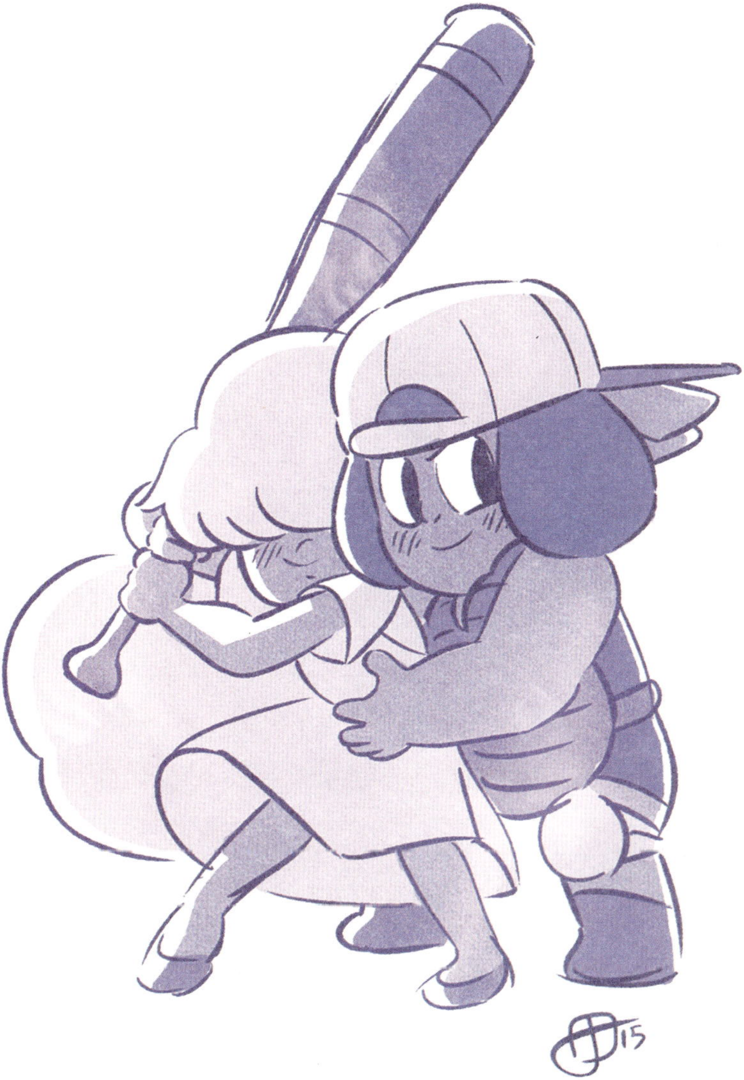

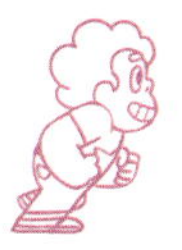

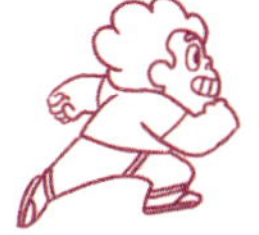

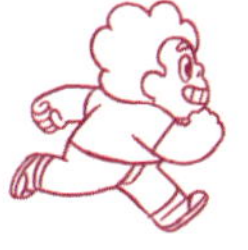

Rebecca Sugar

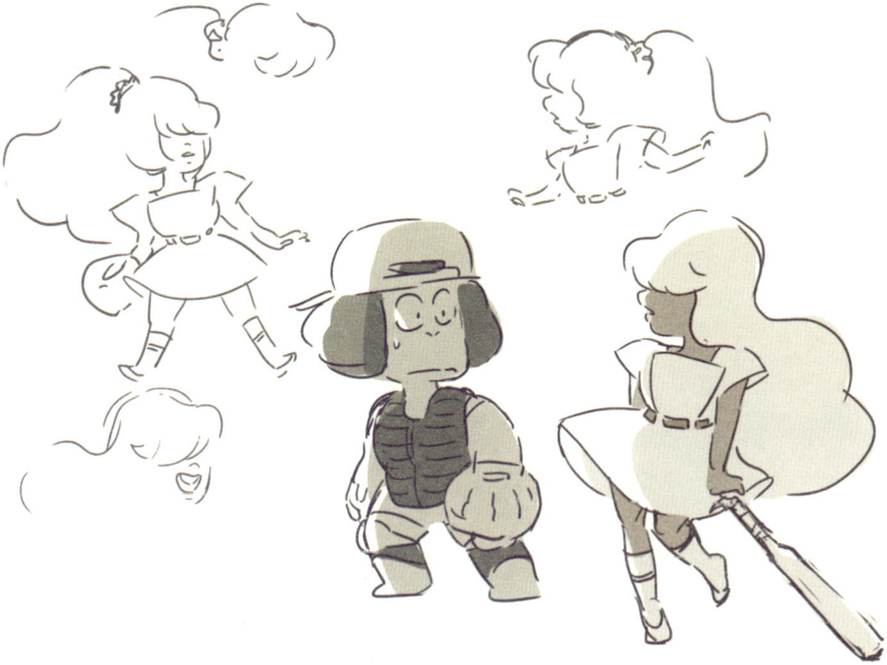

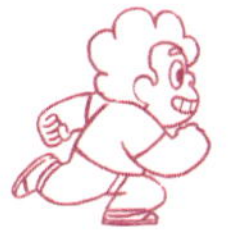

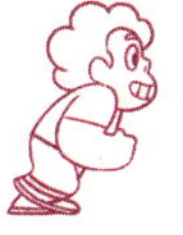

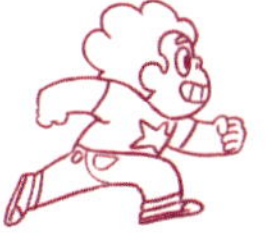

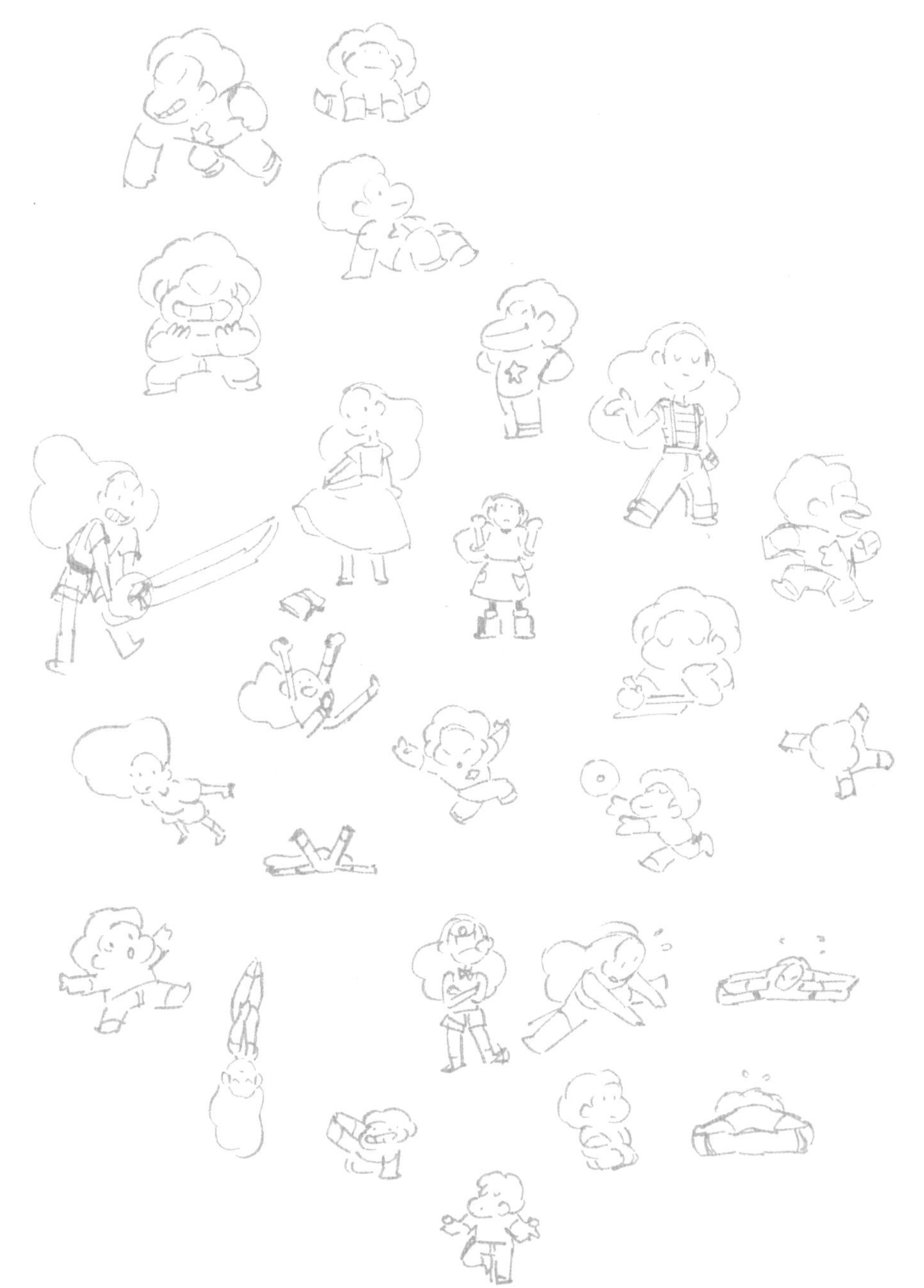

Kat Morris

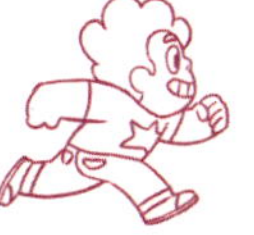

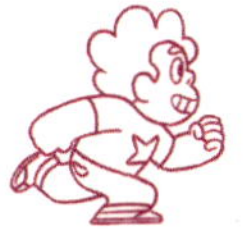

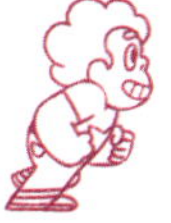

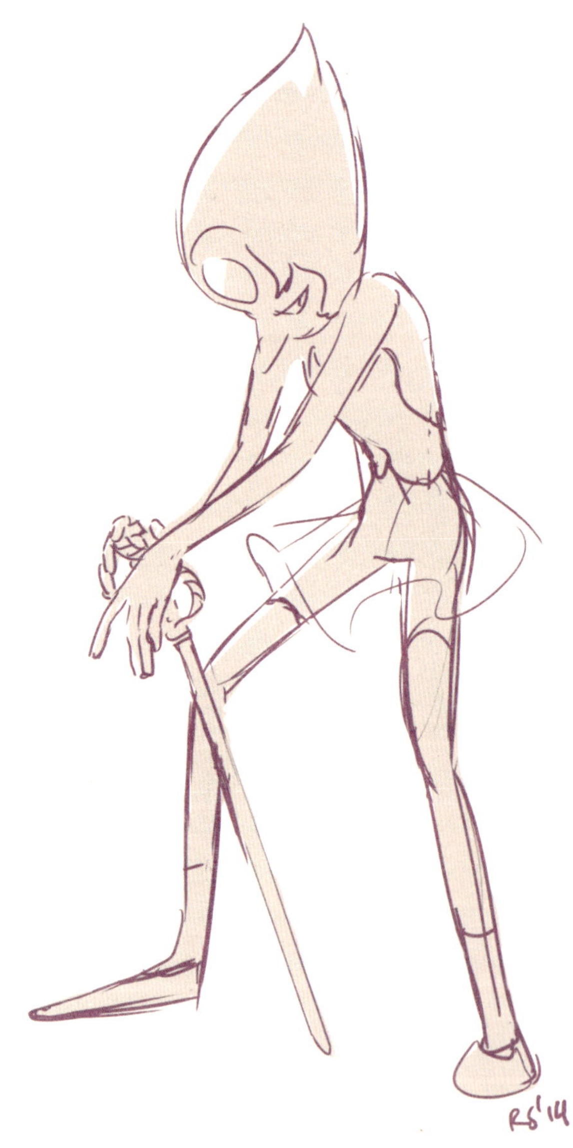

Rebecca Sugar

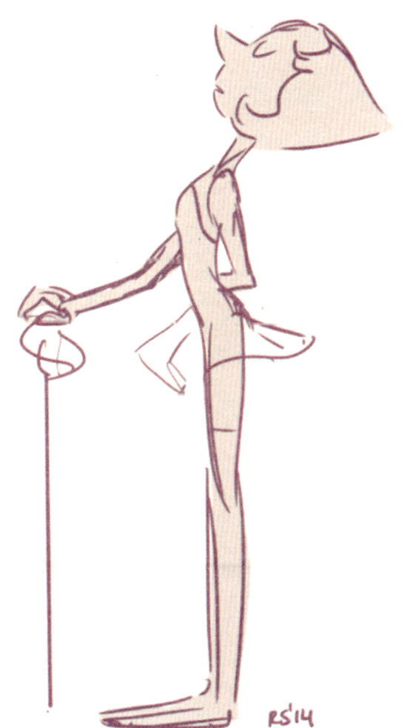
RS'14

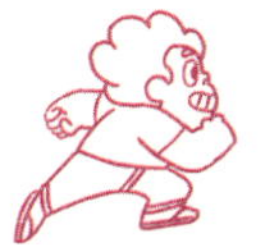

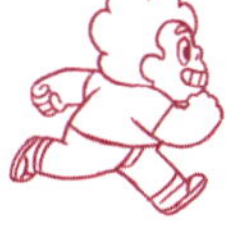

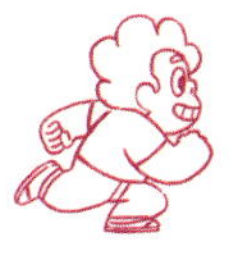

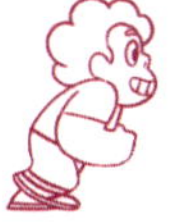

Rebecca Sugar

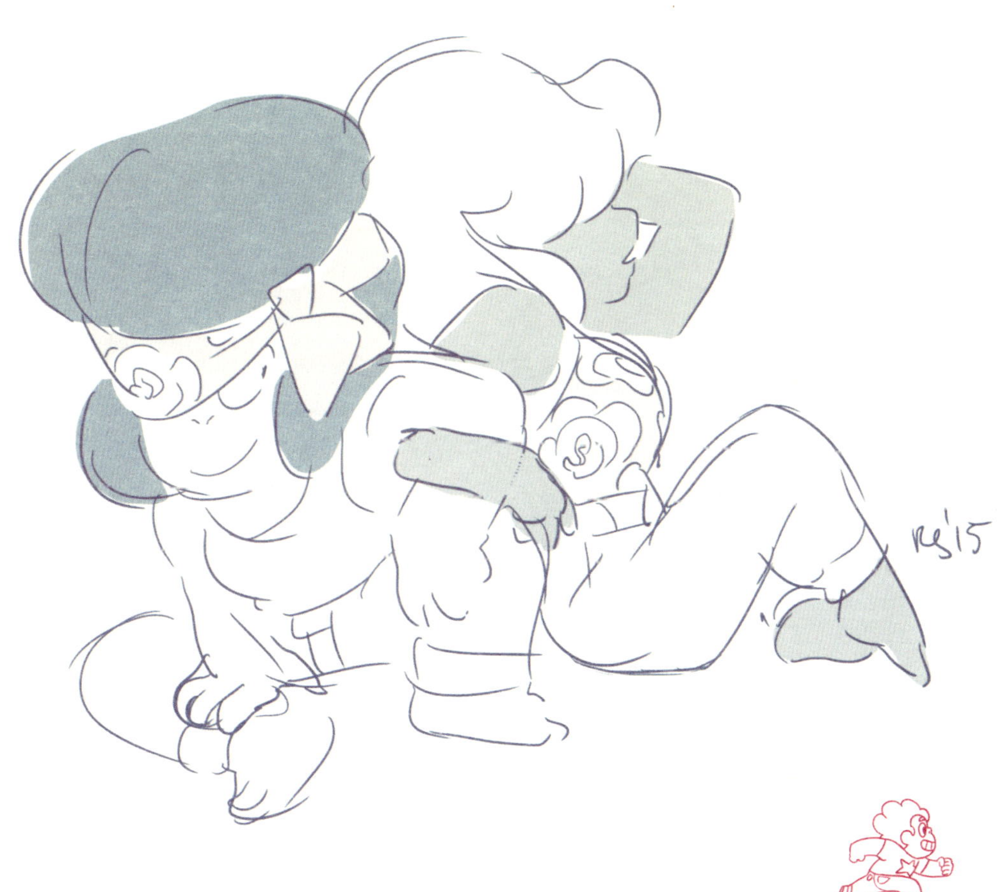

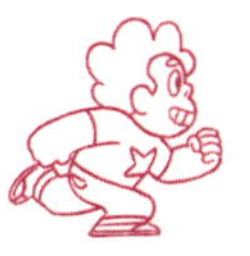

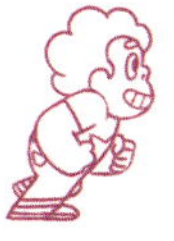

Rebecca Sugar

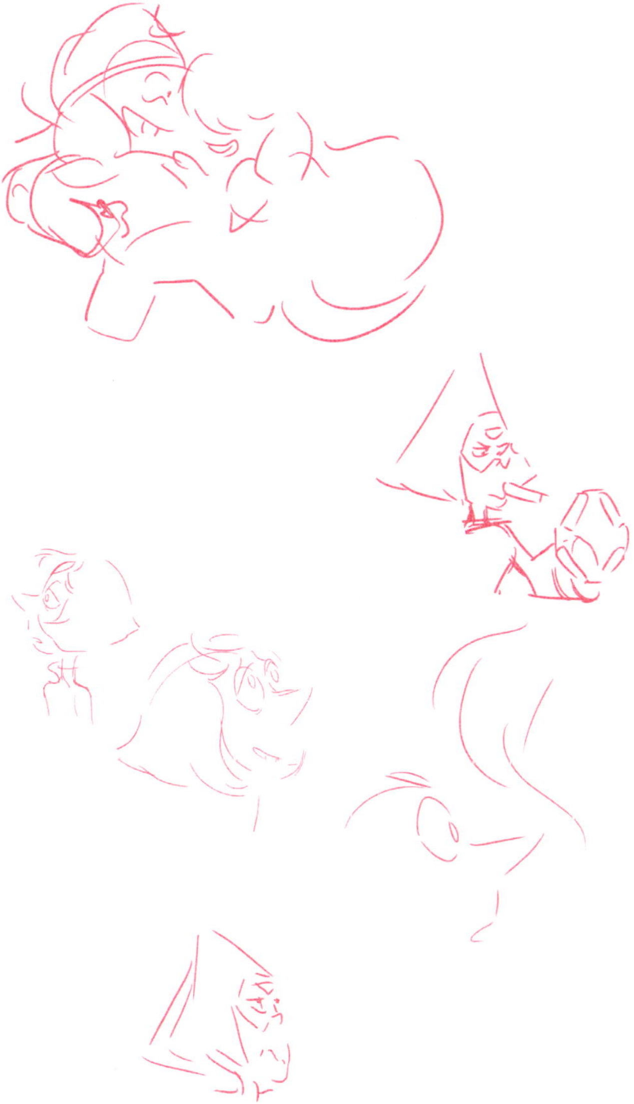

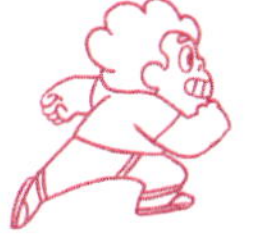

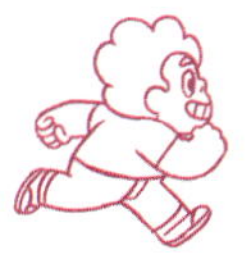

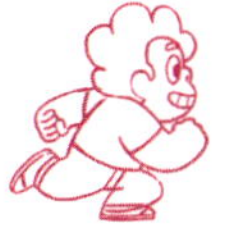

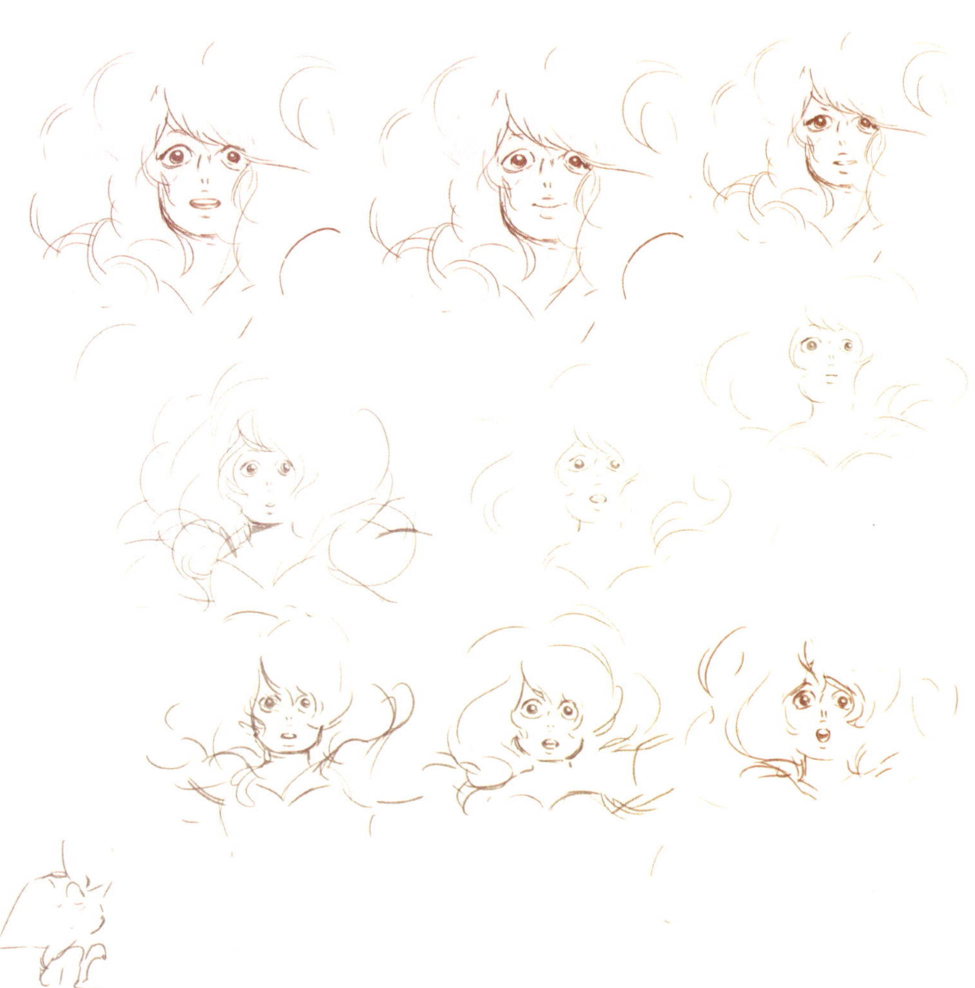

Rebecca Sugar

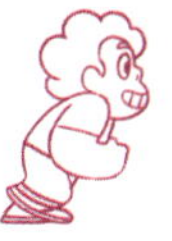

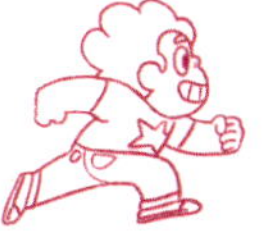

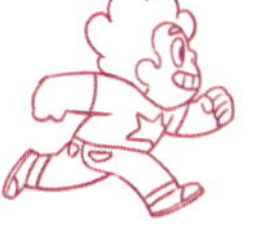

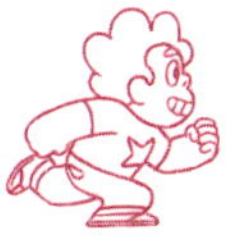

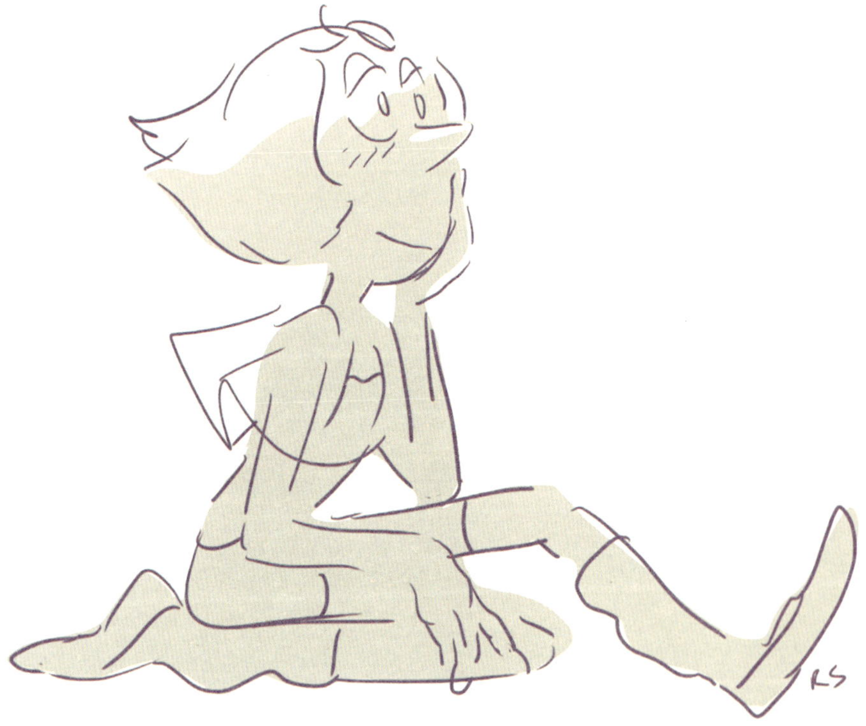

Rebecca Sugar

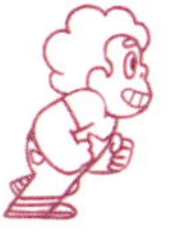

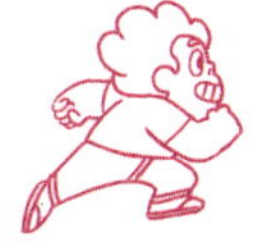

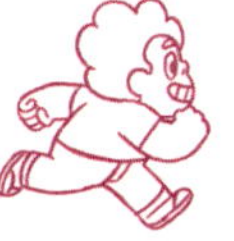

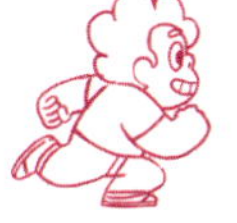

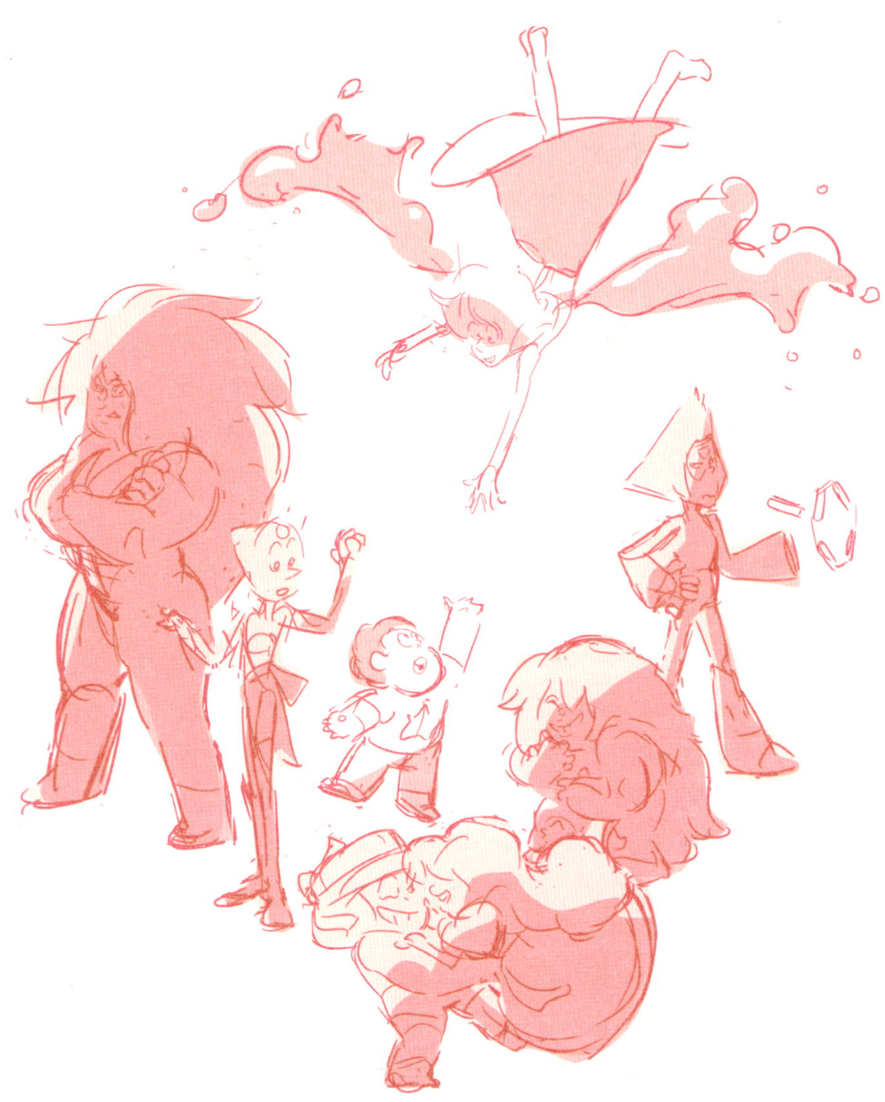

Rebecca Sugar

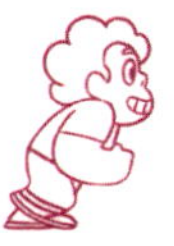

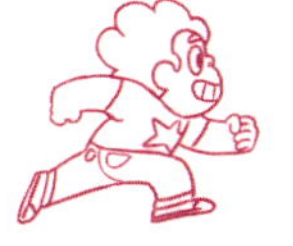

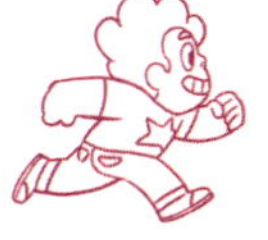

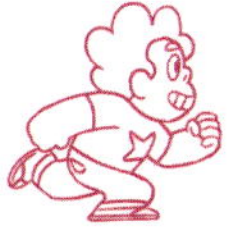

Rebecca Sugar

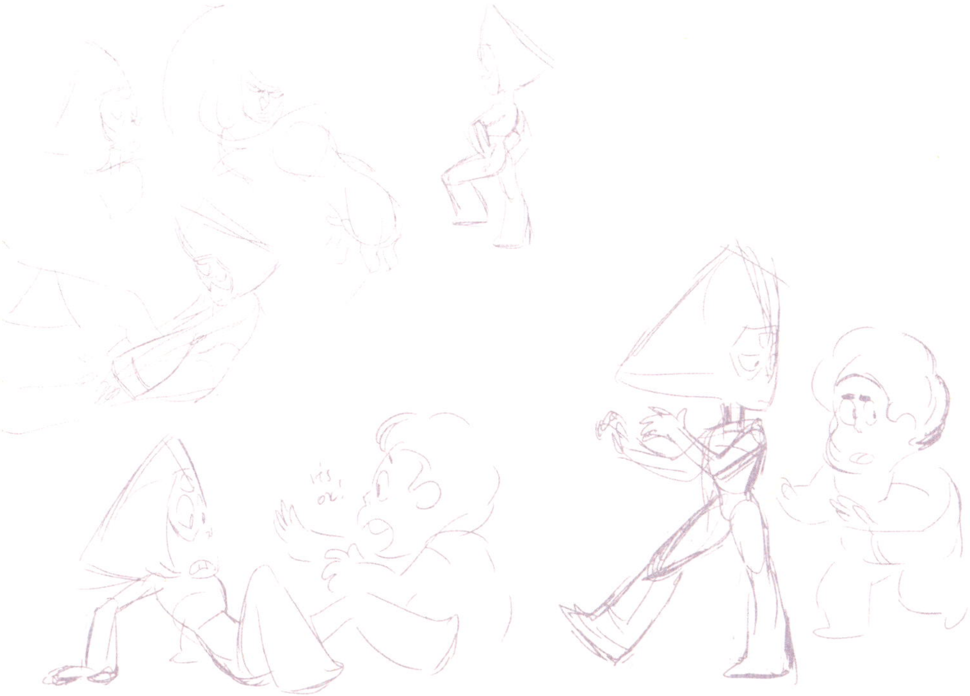

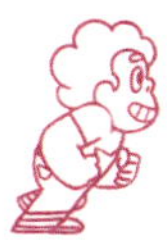

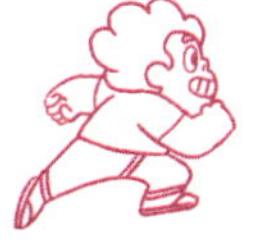

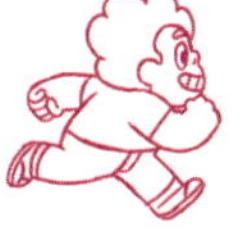

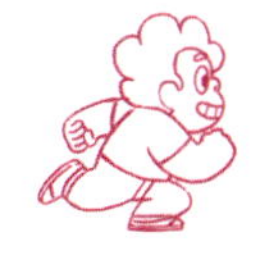

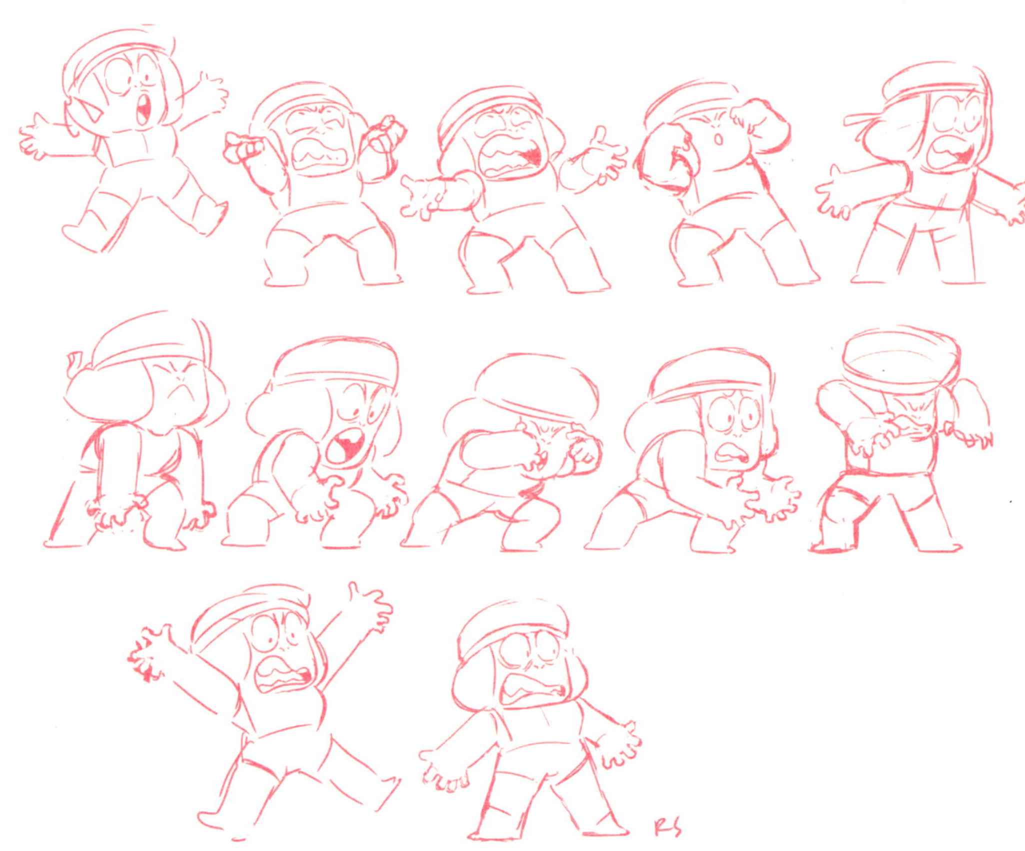

Rebecca Sugar

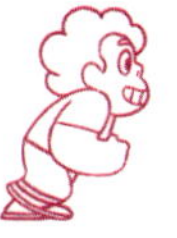

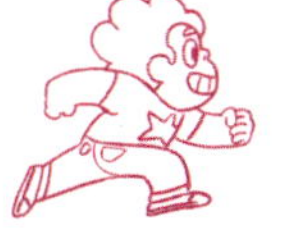

Joe Johnston

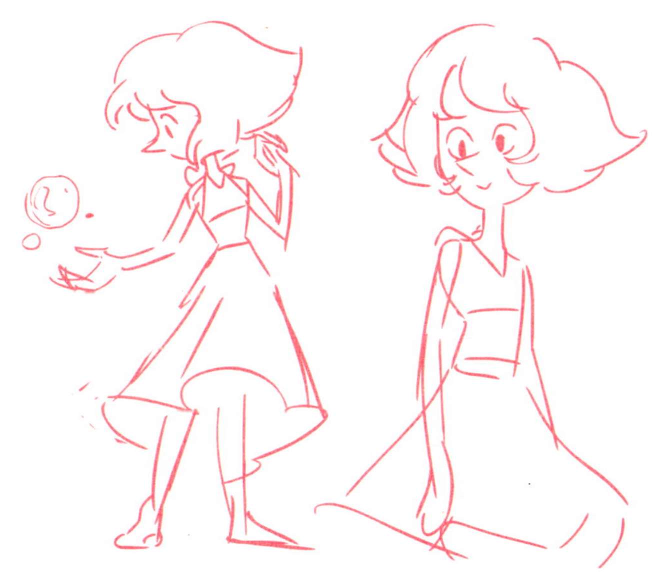

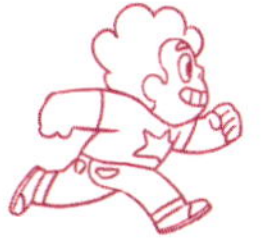

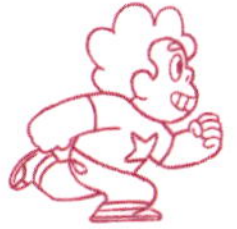

Rebecca Sugar

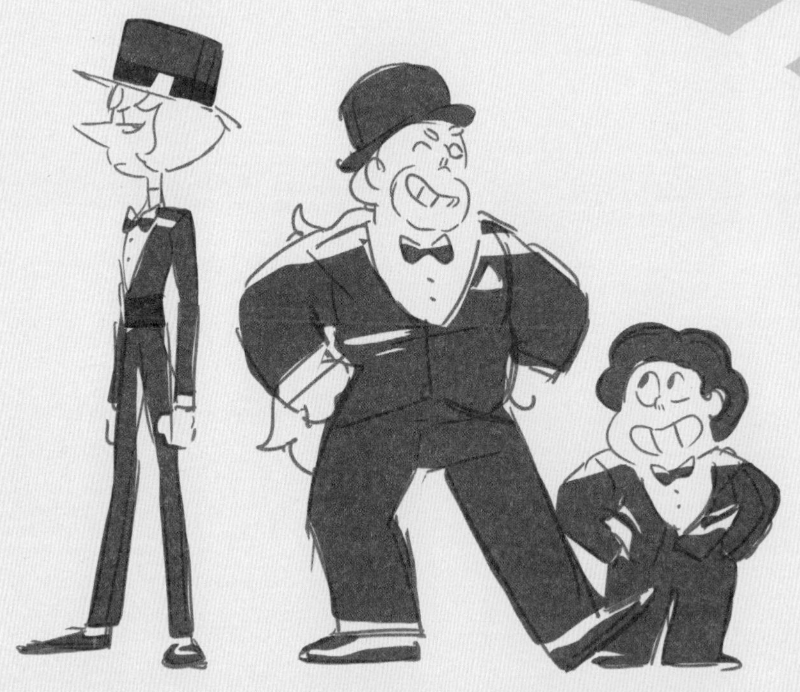

INSIGHTS

www.insighteditions.com

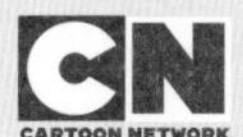

Manufactured in China

10 9 8 7

Artist Credits
Rebecca Sugar, Joe Johnston, Lamar Abrams,
Kat Morris, Jeff Liu

Jeff Liu and Joe Johnston (tiny running Steven on every page)

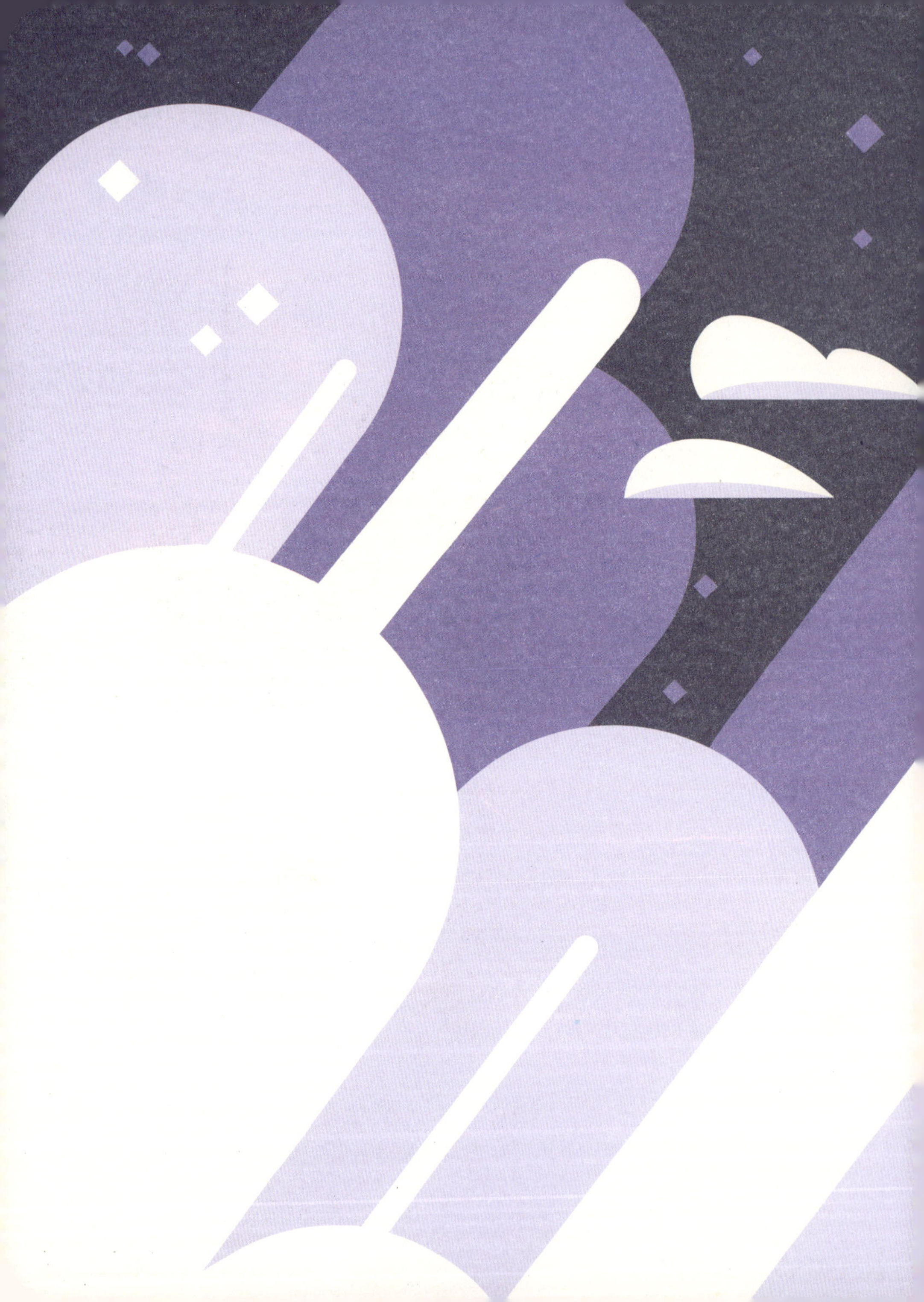